# Spent

**Paul Case**

Lily

Thanks so much for your support! Here's to more film shenanigans!

Patt

**EARTH
ISLAND
BOOKS**

Published by Earth Island Books

Pickforde Lodge

Pickforde Lane

Ticehurst

East Sussex

TN5 7BN


www.earthislandbooks.com


First published by Earth Island Books 2025

ISBN 9781916864504 paperback

ISBN 9781916864511 ebook


Printed and bound by Solopress, Southend

# Contents

# III

*I think my only fear of death*

*is that it may not be the end,*

*that we may be eternal beings*

*and must do all of this again*

Propaghandi, 'Adventures in Zoochosis'

# Spent

I

# This Could Be The Start of Something or Other

crouched on this hillside

throbbing lights

strobe flame over the scampering mass

the bass a natural disaster

sucker punching our spines

the chaos of our pupils

fingers snared

thumb traces knuckle

wrist's beat synching with

my chest's drum roll

these aren't hounds of love Kate

these are fucking wolves

still tearing through the woods

despite all the blows

committed now

this isn't hope

this is certain

connection now forged

countless horizons

to tumble towards


we down our beers

and rise,

ready

## Adam

You remember Adam, right?

It might've been at that expensive warehouse party, or it might've been that free squat party, or it might've been that expensive warehouse party done up to look like a free squat party. The bombs spangled the tips of our tongues as we yelled in the ears of strangers. We staggered, tracing misshapen circles, oblivious to how lost we were.

And later, with cans of extortionate beer warming on the windowsill, knees damp on the floor, we wretched in private and prayed it was still dark enough outside to hide ourselves.

But you remember Adam, right?

It might've been at that post-techno club, where

they didn't play any music, they just chucked a pile of techno albums in the middle of the dance floor and burnt them. We danced and whooped and stomped around the flames like pagans in a harvest fervour.

We stumbled back to Amy's, plastic bags of tinnies jammed in the fridge. We scrambled up the stairs, into the bathroom, locked the door, and in our reflections watched the fashion drain from our faces.

But you remember Adam, right?

It might have been at that awesome house party where we met that girl who said she was a musician recording an album of her sitting near different types of pastry. A tingle as our fingertips touched. We danced, leering, leeching off each other's movements.

And when the slices of morning crept between the curtains, caught in the fug hanging from the ceiling, a feeling sidled up to us, a half memory, of saying the most regretful things.

But you remember Adam, right?

Oh.

You don't remember Adam.

Well this is awkward.

Reminds me, actually, I had this... dream, well, I guess you'd call it a vision, of sorts. We were all sitting in our front room, off our faces, and suddenly the walls started leaking a horrible coloured sludge. The leak grew into a spurt, into a stream, into a geyser. We tried to escape but it was all coming so fast.

We were trapped.

The sludge rose to our knees, hips, chest and, floating in the murk, a lifetime's detritus: screwed up Rizla, ripped baggies, broken wine bottles, crumbs of amphetamine. Soon we were suspended in the sewage of our lives.

As the sludge reached the ceiling we frantically doggy paddled, eyes manic, throats screamed raw. We reached out, held on, dragged each other down...

Soon it would take us entirely.

And the final question that rushed through our heads was:

How did it take so much time to create so much nothing?

## hc

No time to waste –

it swings in,

a meat hook

to the gut.


Stripped,

greased with

toil, flexing

riff bloody,

stick blistered fingers.


Sweeping, majestic landscapes;

endless plains;

trickling streams;

dusks sinking into a vast horizon


can't sound like this.

It's kindled in cities,

dwarfed by concrete valleys,

it distils the

roaring traffic,

ranting drunks,

burning neon,

broken bones,

pulsing sirens,

plundered dreams,

pours them into dirty shot glasses,

downs them

and doesn't flinch.


It's got the clarity of a

straight edge drunk.

Speaks with

gravel-aged youth.

Holds torches to its forbearers

while raging at the world they burned.

Picks scabs

for fresh skin


and scrawls

FUCK THE WORLD I LOVE YOU

on toilet wall tiles.

## Time Travel

forget gender neutral

this pub barely has a ladies'

## Start Today?

I squeeze past two punks at the urinal,

sheen on docs dappled with piss,

baggie squeezed in a sweaty palm.

The cubicle's lock rattles loose. Tap it out,

racked with a derelict gym card.

As I raise my head,

burning with commitment

to the hammered night

and dented days,

the stickers on the tiles

**FCUK NAZIS**

**A.C.A.B**

**BE UNGOVERNABLE**

**NO WAR BUT CLASS WAR**

**RENT STRIKE**

**NO GODS NO MASTERS**

are scratched and peeling.

## Monday After The Festival

The music

      the incandescent thread that weaved
between us in the darkness bound us in the
moment to all human cultural history dubbed our
memories hallowed filled our hopes forced us from
nodding heads to impossible shapes voiced our
belly acid boiled rage cut cauterised healed us made
untamed promises possibilised the future throbbed
damn near split the Earth

      now splintered into
                countless     phones
                        drifting
         home

## In My Wake

I'm the palpitating heart of the party.

I've got a drink in each hand,

I'm grinding right for you,

here to claim the best years of your life.


Go on -

leer at me,

crumbling and dancing across that mirror.

Go on -

try me,

crush me,

chop me up,

brush me away,

dispose of my body,

but my corpse will rise

more fierce than you can ever imagine.


I thicken the air,

stuffing it with jabber

and hollow laughter.

I take time in my hands,

kneading it and stretching it

until minutes become

barren nuclear wastelands

rolling over a horizon;

until hours become

mere glimpses of light.


I'll be your self respect,

your libido,

your love of humanity,

your frailty in the face of certain doom.

I'm the sudden gag at the back of your throat,

the whirling black hole of your dilated pupils,

the white of your knuckles as you grip the toilet

seat,

and as you do the beer run before the shop shuts

I'm the chill that quivers your ribs.

So go on:

shut your curtains tight.

Pull blankets over your heads

like children hiding from rapacious monsters,

whisper through parched pale lips,

but I'll come creeping in with the slabs of dawn

and rise with the goosebumps that pepper your

flesh.

I'll annihilate your tomorrow

and the next day if I'm lucky,

and birds will scatter the skies

when you scream my name.


And then I'm gone –

leaving you crawling out the hole

that yawns in my wake.

## Bridges

They push forward, vibrating in their ecstatic skirmish, voices unified over gang choruses, clenched fists raised toward the ceiling.

They might glimpse us, cusp of the stage lights' sweep, hidden like old toys. We'll be softly nodding our heads to the beat, plastic pints dribbling foam over our hands, already dreading tomorrow's hangover.

Maybe later we'll build a bridge, fashioned from powders and wreathes of cigarette smoke; bolstered by shots and chats that go nowhere. But it'll crumble under the light, and our futures will fork like a wishbone.

## Intrusion

An exhumation

deep in my gut.

My wasted time,

back from the dead,

crawling up to greet me.

## Blowing Up

The mandy is cheap.

A restless heat

with no release.

Teeth gyrating,

our baccy-stained fingers

clench cans

and flex

in and out of fists

under a strobe-blistered sky.

Our voices burnt hoarse

from cigarettes and

raging beats.

The snare on our tongues,

the bass in our guts.

My boots spin away,

desperate for a place

where the night ends.

You grab my hoody
in a dubstep drop.

Pure filth.

There's no escape
til the pigs come.

## Drink Alone

Sweep through the supermarket

to the tinkle of muzak and the striplight buzz

beelining to the reduced section.

There's the battered multipack of Tennent's

or the bruised dark fruits Strongbow,

sellotaped together

on the verge of collapse,

which reminds us

that we don't have to worry about what anyone

thinks

because we're going to

drink alone.

So we get the Tennent's and the Strongbow

- y'know, just in case -

and do what must be done

to galvanise those few snatches of nothing

as we drink alone,

then let time shrink until only traces remain

on the fringes of history.

Ruins from a self-destructed civilisation.


Drink alone.

And none of our so-called mates are badgering us

to get our round in or whinging that they're skint

or acting like twats or getting in fights.

No.

It's quiet here.

But we message them anyway.

Two blue ticks like frozen lightning bolts,

a hope that never quite explodes.


Drink alone.

Tears will spring at some point,

some memory or feeling bobbing around.

We'll watch it flail for a while

but it'll sink eventually.

Drowned. Forgotten.

And we'll wonder what all the fuss was about
because everything's better now
or at least, it exists a bit less.

Drink alone.
A blurred confusion comes over us.
Everything is fine though:
ride the confusion, go wherever it takes us,
just remember we'll always end up where we
began:

drinking alone,
swaddled in misery and comfort,
slumped on the sofa,
trying to force the stars into alignment,
a map of cosmic justice,
but we lose our grip and they spin in space
til they're gone, gone, gone.

We won't sleep. We'll transcend

to a place where nothing dreams

and nothing lives.

A black cloak

to hide us away,

and it's so perfect.

## Caught, Drunk In Charge of an Existence

Sorry.

It's just a one off.

Won't happen again.

## Champagne

Throttle the bottle's neck

in an icy grip,

raise it and cherish

the shudder as it


smashes,

shards of glass and booze

spattering my cheek,


bubbling creeks merge

into furious frothing lakes,

a million undulating eyes

pleading forgiveness as they float away,


but I will be pitiless

and walk away

victorious.

## Knowledge

Always wondered how you end up one of those
faceless men drinking deep at the bar as Saturday
night swirls about them.

Now I know.

# Purge

hangover swinging heavy, a wrecking ball
smashing my guts, send you the text as I march
down the high street. clouds with grey underbellies
gather, cars pass, waving shadows up and down
brick walls, appended by a burst of black wings,
vapourised by naked light,

and I wake in the pub to the electric scream of slot
machines, there's others dotted about but we're
observing the solemn, respectful silence that late
morning drinking commands, I peer up, out of the
window: clouds heavier, darker, grumbling,

and I've got a taste for it again now, fuck it, get
another pint, try to be at peace with it like that
scabrous barfly, staring into the blank abyss of his
beer, but every time the pub door opens there's a
flit of cardiac arrest, and in that brief fall, that tiny

death, my stout is stuffed with black feathers, and,
this atonement attested, I'm led back to you and
the burst yolks of poached eggs with spinach on
sourdough bread at pricey cafes

and these clouds are streaked raven feather, your
charcoal hair rippling across our sleep-crinkled
pillows, and they shake the first sprinkles of rain,
the concrete at my feet fading into quivering grass,
but I press on with squishing steps, dusk brushed
away, stars throb as the clouds strobe, haul myself
up some hill, some mountain, it's pissing down, a
bone crack of thunder, a serrated bolt fractures the
sky, and legs aching, haul myself up, mud and
sodden grass in my fists,

and I reach the top, before me is a canvas of pure
black pinned with the city's dying lights smudged
by the downpour, all I feel is a smallness, curled
foetal and shaking with fear,

I say your name, over and over, keeping it warm on

my lips but it's smothered by the storm's groan, so

I'm screaming it, a mantra burning my throat


and everything stops.


It's a clear, blazing morning


the city has disappeared, sunken under the spread

of lucent green meadow that's in its place


a raven caws, blasts past me, vanishing into the

aching bright blue


my phone vibrates


I know it's your reply, and forgiveness will never

come.

**II**

# Dead White Anarchists

By the time he was twenty, Emile Henry had decided he was an anarchist. He had flirted with a couple of different movements in the past, like socialism and spiritualism, but both left him feeling a bit cold. His love of liberty – of total liberty – didn't exactly chime with the restrictive offerings from the left wing political groups; and his love of science - of rationality - quickly dispatched any curiosity in ghosts after a few séances. He wanted something more grounded, more visceral, more final.

By the flicker of candlelight – crammed into his tiny bedroom, which was crammed into a tiny house, which was crammed into the one of the many slums that orbited the fiery electric glow of Paris' city centre – he avidly gorged on any anarchist literature he could get his hands on: Mikhail Bakunin, Errico Malatesta, Peter

Kropotkin, Johann Most, Emile Pouget...

Pierre-Joseph Proudhon's famous words were a bolting epiphany to Emile:

*To be governed is to be watched over, inspected, spied on, directed, legislated at, regulated, docketed, indoctrinated, preached at, controlled, assessed, weighed, censored, ordered about, by men who have neither the right, nor the knowledge, nor the virtue. ... To be governed is to be at every operation, at every transaction, noted, registered, enrolled, taxed, stamped, measured, numbered, assessed, licensed, authorized, admonished, forbidden, reformed, corrected, punished. It is, under the pretext of public utility, and in the name of the general interest, to be placed under contribution, trained, ransomed, exploited, monopolized, extorted, squeezed, mystified, robbed; then, at the slightest resistance, the first word of complaint, to be repressed, fined, despised, harassed, tracked, abused, clubbed, disarmed, choked,*

*imprisoned, judged, condemned, shot, deported,*
*sacrificed, sold, betrayed; and, to crown all, mocked,*
*ridiculed, outraged, dishonoured. That is government;*
*that is its justice; that is its morality.*


This is what he had been waiting for. Death had hung over him in so many fragmented, shadowy forms all his life but these words... they bound it all together. His dad had died when he was nine. Lead poisoning from working in the copper mines, the doctor had said. Emile remembered clutching his Mum's hand at the funeral, their fingers twitching together in grief as the priest's words burbled into the breeze.

His Mum and Dad, in turn, had been part of the Paris Commune of 1871 – a revolution! – where, for just over two months, the workers had taken over the city. The story had been whispered to Emile so many times that it felt like a phantom limb on a memory. And he also remembered being told about the terrible fall of the Commune – the French army storming Paris and massacring twenty five thousand people in a week.

A crass warning to the future: *don't ever try this again.*

*

And now, in 1892, he witnessed his inheritance in the crimes of corrupt politicians and cutthroat capitalists every day in the slums: open sewers that festered with disease; people forced to work twelve, fourteen, sixteen hour days for starvation wages and that's if they could find work at all. And sometimes, on his way to work, he saw tiny bodies covered in filthy sheets.

And those who fed off this death, growing fat from this cannibalism, were alive – they were always so fucking alive, weren't they? - drinking their wine, smugly shielded by the law. Capitalism and the State. Hand in hand.

The face of the world had been ripped off,

revealing to Emile nothing but insanity and gore underneath– the eyes rolling meaninglessly in their sockets, and the muscle and sinew pulling as the naked mouth screamed and screamed.

*

Around that time, if you were so inclined and knew where to look or where to steal it from, getting hold of the stuff to make bombs was actually pretty easy. And crinkled pamphlets were surreptitiously passed around that detailed exactly how to make one.

In March 1892 a man named Ravachol, with some accomplices, placed two bombs in Paris. His targets: a judge and a prosecuting attorney who were involved in the case against some wrongfully arrested anarchists. Everyone knew they were going to push for the death penalty. Ravachol wanted to get there first.

The bombs went off.

His targets?

Unscathed.

He was arrested at a restaurant a few days later. He slipped up, openly chatting about anarchism with a waiter when his face was all over the papers. The waiter put two and two together and made the call. Apparently, it took ten police to drag Ravachol to the ground.

He was sentenced to death.

A couple of weeks after his execution, there was an anarchist meeting in a café in Paris. Ravachol's name - his bombings, his defiant arrest, his passionate defence speech, his head rolling on the boards – underpinned every conversation, and there was a lick of tension to the air, an undertow of anger, the kind of anger that only the stormy alchemy of cheap gin and burgeoning vengeance can conjure up.

A speaker was on the stage - a stout man with a tiny black moustache.

'Look I, um, I hate the rich, the justice system,

the police, the State, as much as anyone here, but er, it has to be said, lionising Ravachol would be a mistake.'

Silence. Deathly silence. A hundred eyes pinning him to the wall.

"What we need is, um — "he looked down at the notes in his shaking hand — "mass mobilised action from workers to fight capitalism…"

Unsettled grumblings from the audience. They'd heard this stuff for too long. Meeting after meeting after god damn meeting. And here they still were — still 'organising', still wading through the shit of Paris for pennies, still listening to people like… what the hell was his name again?

As he began his undoubtedly really long recommended reading list just in case you wanted to brush up on your anarcho-syndicalist theory, someone yelled from the back:

'FUCK YOUR THEORY! WE NEED ACTION NOW!'

Pockets of cheers from the audience.

The speaker buckled a little, but refused to relent.

'And also, um... this is quite interesting, if you're into that sort of thing, I heartily recommend this pamphlet. Admittedly it's a little dry in parts, but I think it really has some valuable...'

A woman at the front shot up, her face scarlet with booze and rage.

'BLOW THE BASTARDS UP!'

'Look Madam – and Sir don't think I didn't hear you – I think you'll find everyone has the right to have their say and...'

From somewhere in the audience, a screwed up bit of paper soared through the air and hit the speaker in the forehead, followed by a cry of 'VIVA RAVACHOL!'

The chant swept through the audience, backed by clapping hands and stamping feet:

'VIVA RAVACHOL! VIVA RAVACHOL! VIVA RAVACHOL!'

Under this hail of cries, the speaker was crushed. He folded up his notes, put them in his pocket and shuffled offstage with the little dignity he could take with him.

He was forgotten as soon as the next speaker took to the stage – a young man, who passionately extolled the virtues of the great leveller of their time: dynamite. The audience hung on his every word, nodding sagely along to every damning proclamation, occasionally possessed by a swelling righteousness, standing and yelling: 'DEATH TO THE BOURGEOISIE!'

As the weeks wore on, the myth of Ravachol was quickly spun: a poor man pushed down by HIS poverty, shoved to the margins and striking back against a system that destroyed him and others like him. And the articles, poems, songs and stories that poured from pens and mouths and on to the streets quickly twisted into war cries for bloody revenge.

As Emile quietly soaked all this in he imagined

himself on a raft, floating down a river of spilt blood and broken bones towards a cavernous black from which these war cries swelled and died and swelled again. Powerless to stop the current but prepared to meet any horrors that came his way.

He already knew who the enemies were. But now he realised they had names, they had faces.... and they had addresses.

He was glad that, while he had never been unsociable exactly, he had kept a certain distance from people. This would make everything much, much easier.

*

The horse drawn carriage bumped and juddered over the cobblestoned boulevards of central Paris and Emile, the only passenger, was nervous.

But he wasn't nervous for the reasons you or I would probably be nervous in his situation. For example, he wasn't nervous about killing people. He'd briefly considered the innocent and the loss of life but... what the does innocence even mean in this crooked, decaying world? What does life even mean when children just down the road are starving and cold while the wealthy are warmed by their brandy and log fires?

So he wasn't nervous about that.

And he wasn't nervous about being caught, arrested, interrogated and, most likely, executed either. Obviously, he would prefer it if these things didn't happen... but he was ready. He had to be. He reasoned that you don't go into war without facing the possibility of your own destruction.

No. He was nervous about not hitting his target. He'd worked meticulously until dawn. Potassium chloride and a touch of sodium mixed up in one compartment of a tin, and in the other compartment was some water, and if the tin was disturbed the mix would come into contact with water and then...

He clutched the package tight against his chest.

If it went off now, it would kill him, the horse, the driver, a few bystanders, and the thought of his hard work being reduced to a stupid mistake, and his revolutionary obituary ending with him blowing himself up, really annoyed him. History was full of footnote fuckwits and Emile refused to be one of them.

He asked the driver to stop a block away from the Carmaux Mining Company offices.

Okay, a bit of background: The Carmaux Mining Company had recently crushed a miner's strike, and while the strikers had dug their heels in for three months, the union funds had run dry, the army had intimidated them, and eventually they were forced to go back to work, down the mines.

Emile thought of his Dad.

He wanted to show the strikers, the unions, the mining company, Paris, France, no – fuck it – the world – the true face of class war, with all the sloganeering and posturing boiled off, and the remnants distilled into pure violent reaction.

He stood outside the grand glass doors that led into the building.

It's worth mentioning at this point that Emile wasn't a Ravachol – a ragged figure from the margins invading the high society that ignored him. No. While broke, Emile was firmly part of the middle classes, and had all the attending confidence that meant he could shift around the world of the affluent unnoticed.

And it's with this confidence that he pushed open the grand glass door, nodded hello to the concierge who nodded hello back, walked up the stairs to the mezzanine, laid his package outside the door of the mining company office, walked back down the stairs, nodded goodbye to the concierge who nodded goodbye back, pushed open the glass door and slipped into the sunlight.

The news was all over Paris by the end of the day: Package Found Outside Carmaux Mining Company

Offices. Given the political climate it seemed prudent to call the police and two diligent police officers went to assess the situation and reasoned that the best thing to do was pick up the package and take it down to the station. But as soon as they laid it on the table to be inspected...

Five police dead.

It took days to scrape the remains from the walls.

The news awed, stunned, shocked or appalled Paris, depending on who you asked.

And no one knew who did it.

*

Emile needed to get out of Paris fast. And there was only one place he could reasonably go. And while London didn't interest Emile particularly, it did have its bonuses. For example, he didn't even need a passport to get there, and he could easily squirrel himself away in the radical enclaves of Fitzrovia or Soho that were stuffed with exiled European dissidents.

That's how Emile found himself in London, crashing on people's floors, surrounded by snoring émigrés.

He was bored. Really bored. But he accepted that boredom was a necessary part of war. He drifted around, wandered the streets, meandered in his own thoughts. He went to a few bohemian hang outs, talked books, skirted around the fringes of his interests but was careful not to talk too much – there were turncoats everywhere. If the subject of the Paris police station bombing came up, he would feign innocence and interest until he found a moment where he could quietly and politely slip away.

December, 1893. And Emile was still in London, sitting in a pub, nursing a pint. He'd just heard news of another anarchist bombing in Paris. A man named Auguste Vaillant, enraged by Ravachol's execution, had made a bomb, snuck into the

Parliament's Chamber of Deputies when they were in session and thrown it at the politicians. No one was seriously hurt and he was arrested on the spot.

While Emile was glad that the war was continuing in his absence, he thought that if you were going to go through the bother of making a bomb, sneaking into the Parliament's Chamber of Deputies and throwing it at politicians, you may as well take a few of the bastards out. He'd heard the device was weak. This is the problem, Emile thought, when people don't have a decent grounding in chemistry.

He mulled it all over.

He was going to continue his war, no doubt about that. But Paris would be on red alert now. The police would be swooping down: more spies, more raids, more interrogations. And, even if they didn't know he was responsible for the Paris police station bombing, he was a known anarchist, and the fact they couldn't find him would make them suspicious. They'd probably visit his old work, maybe even his family...

He imagined a heavy boot kicking down the door of his Mum's house, long shadows stretching over her terrified face, and the thought made Emile ball his hands up so tight that his nails drove into his palm.

No. This is what they want: to use their brutality to make you feel guilty, to drag you out of hiding...

No. No surrender.

Emile felt a dry tightness in his throat, and washed it away with the remaining dregs of his beer. Then he ordered another.

Then another.

And then another.

*

'OI!'

Emile rose his head and realised he was completely and utterly hammered. A red faced barman filled his view, his thick fingers pressing down on the table.

'Home time now, go on, fuck off.'

Emile desperately wanted to reconcile the situation, but everything that came out of his mouth was just fragmented gibberish.

The barman rolled his eyes, strode behind Emile, lifted him by his armpits and tossed him out onto the street. The slam of the heavy wooden door and the clank of the massive metal lock cut through the boozy fog that plumed in his mind.

He had no idea where he was. But he did know, somewhere in the dim, pissed workings of his mind, that he was drunk. It was dark. And it was cold. And therefore he wasn't supposed to be here, he was supposed to be... somewhere else.

So off he staggered into the unknown, tracing mapless routes to a fictional home, stumbling over cobblestones, muttering half-formed curses to himself.

After a little while of this, he felt a surge in his

gut. In panicked instinct, he spun around to face the wall, bowed his head, dry heaving a couple of times before the cathartic geyser spewed out, wet chunks splattering the wall and his trousers and his shoes.

When he had finished, he remained bent over, spluttering and spitting the acid burn from his throat, tears flecked with relieved tears, heart pounding in his chest, heavy breath roaring in his ears.

As he calmed, sobering up a little, his heart beat slowing, the roaring ebbed away, and was replaced by something entirely different.

A dull, repetitive, low, throbbing buzz, completely alien to Emile, but he could feel its nameless power vibrating the bricks against his fingertips. It was the kind of sound he imagined the awesome machines in science fiction novels would make, the thrilling hum of the future, and it was coming from an alleyway just around the corner and, entranced, he followed the sound, enveloping himself in the alleyway's dankness, and this was where the sound was loudest, a booming, crushing thud that shook Emile's bones.

He found himself outside a ramshackle building that seemed to stretch endlessly up into the night sky. The only lights came from windows four stories up, bleeding a magical plethora of colours into the air, occasionally delving into a split second of darkness before exploding into a rapid flicker of blinding black and white, all working in perfect symphony with the sound. Emile gazed up at them, utterly transfixed.

His reverie was broken by a metal door at the side of the building bursting open and the sound rushed out like a gale, like a scream from an electronic netherworld, and a gaggle of dark figures spilled out after it, reeking of sweat and cigarettes and booze. They whisked past Emile and vanished as quickly as they'd appeared, their cackles lingering in the air for a second before being absorbed by the raging noise.

The metal door hung open, light and smoke and noise, pure vicious sensation, pouring out. Emile peered in. He was sober enough to be slightly terrified, but drunk enough to obey the yank of curiosity within him.

He also could've also done with another beer.

So, with that in mind, he stepped in.

*

Emile was lost in the heat and clamour immediately. He spun around to escape, but the metal door had been swallowed up by the vast crowd that swarmed around him, a demented carousel of screeching and yelling and singing, all barely audible under the blistering beating sound that trembled the foundations of the building. Propelled by the insanity, he was tumbled down some corridor, and on his way he could just about make out words that seemed to be scarred into the walls:

ANNIHILATE THE STATE

DEATH 2 COPS

TOTAL FUCKING FREEDOM

Emile had only a moment to think what this meant before he was forced on, deeper and deeper into this frenzied warren. Panic seized his lungs, squeezing them in staccato bursts, his skull tightened against his brain, pressure rising, drowning in terror before he was spewed out into a vast space, a wall of sound crashing over him, each beat a brick smashing him in the face. Despite the raging noise, he was thankful to be alive, and he sucked this new space into his parched lungs, but on looking up a new madness presented itself.

A massive crowd of people, moving in jerky rhythms, limbs flailing, heads snapping backwards and forwards, skin glowing and glistening, silhouettes gyrating in some Hellish parody of fucking against the lasers. Emile looked for a way out but he knew it was impossible, he knew all the exits had been subsumed by this shape shifting place, looping around and around, controlled only by the fury of the crowd, time and space rendered to nothing, the only ritual being that there were no rituals, everything surrendered to the nihilism of the moment.

He ran, bouncing between bodies, slipping and sliding on the drenched floor, pleading for it all to just fucking STOP STOP STOP STOP STOP FUCKING STOP until, he found himself at something like a bar, and behind the bar was a half naked man, ears and nose robed with steel. Emile leant in, screaming in a garbled French and English patois, saying he thought was losing his mind and he didn't know if he was going to get it back.

The barman furrowed his brow, reached under the counter, and placed a can of extra strong Polish lager between them, holding up two fingers to indicate the price.

Emile leaned in to scream again but was stopped by a fist appearing between them, one of the knuckles crowned with a small pile of white powder. As the barman bent his head and snorted it up, Emile seized his opportunity, grabbed the beer and vanished into the crowd.

He found a space on the edge of the pandemonium where he could observe the arrhythmic flow of bodies exploding into a thousand fragments before coalescing in a breath. Steam rose off them, the heat contagious, and sweat trickled down the back of Emile's neck. He drained his beer. He wanted more, but knew he couldn't go back to the bar now. As he considered his options he noticed, on a shelf next to him, an abandoned can of beer. He glanced around for a potential owner – there was no one – picked it up, shook it – three quarters full – and took a sip.

Warm. Disgusting. But it was booze.

That's how Emile passed the next couple of

hours: fruitlessly attempting to out drink insanity, downing abandoned beers. Some were cold and refreshing; others a bit flat and tepid; a minority had cigarette butts at the bottom that made Emile gag as he they slipped down his throat but he didn't care. He just wanted to cope, or manage, or obliterate himself. Whatever.

After an unknown slice of time falling down shapeless corridors and up meaningless stairs, seemed for hours, days, weeks, time elastic, eventually he stumbled into a small room away from the chaos, the music muted back to that dull thud.

People were sprawled everywhere – on armchairs and sofas and on the floor. Some kissing madly, some in varying catatonic states, yet others chatted animatedly, cigarettes disappearing and reappearing in rushed breaths, everyone dabbing at tiny bags, snorting at lines of powder from any available surface but Emile was too exhausted to care any more, the idea of rest, of sleep, of a dreamless black. He slumped into an armchair, the room spinning.

'You alright?'

Emile looked up. A young, olive-skinned woman, with tattoos snaking up her arms and dreads cascading down her back, was speaking to him. He thought her eyes looked bizarre, the pupils nearly blotting out all the whiteness. He felt he was staring into the centre of the universe.

This is Alicia. Alicia had been pub crawling all day with a couple of friends on their way to this South London squat party, dipping into their MDMA and acid stash on the way, and as soon as she had arrived her friends disappeared into the chaos and now, at this point in her intoxication, the empathy rushing through her bloodstream, she just felt the desperate need for this hammered stressed out guy to be on her level.

She reached into her bra and took out out a tiny

bit of cardboard – a tab of acid – tore it in half and handed one half to Emile. He stared at the piece of cardboard utterly perplexed. Alicia grinned and showed how to take it by placing it on the tip of her pierced tongue and swallowing. Emile held the piece of cardboard between his fingers. Whatever, he thought. Come on. Keep the madness coming. Whatever the hell this is, I can take it. He mimicked her and put his head in his hands.

After about an hour, things really began to fall apart.

He drifted away from Alicia, dragged by the terrible power of this place, eyelid slits of light expanding, stretching into a horizon, over which a dawn blistered and broke, spilling out dark rainbows, laser lit night-time rivers, and it was all so strange and beautiful and awful that Emile could nothing but stand there and take it, that sound – that dull thud - had seemed aeons away, but now it was back, growing into a bludgeoning white roar as silhouetted figures twisted and pirouetted around him, and skulls, skulls of faces he knew he recognised, blasted out of the darkness before receding once more, his lungs gave way, crushed, buried alive under this psychosis, his clothes now soaked with sweat, weighed him down, impeding his movements, snaring his liberty, so he ripped them off, allowing the soggy garments to slap the floor, and naked he strode on, his heart a fist pounding his rib cage, he knew the bones were breaking, and no one can hold back history he thought, no one can hold back history but we can destroy it and we can create it but you have to know your place in all this fucking mess and it was then he saw the words, the terrible words burnt into the wall, bordered with licking flames and billowing smoke that rose into invisible ceiling, and they read:

THIS

IS

ANARCHY

Emile froze, reading the words over and over, taking in the carnage around him, 'no, no, no this can't be anarchy this can't be anarchy this can't be anarchy' and he knew the past was coming for him, he could feel it, shredding the present into tiny invisible fragments behind him, and in his final moments, naked, he fell to his knees, bent his head down to the sticky floor, breathed in the stench of a wrecked wasted future, and he screamed. He screamed for the Paris Commune, he screamed for his Mum and Dad, he screamed for Ravachol and Auguste Vaillant, and he screamed for all the dead. And he screamed for the world that was never was.

Then the past washed over him.

*

When Emile woke, it was February 12th, 1894, and he was sitting in the Café Terminus in central Paris. He let the normality sink in: the small round table; the half finished beer; the smouldering cigar perched on the ashtray, and, beyond that, the band that had just kicked up a waltz; the music drifting into the fog of smoke and perfume that rose from men in suits and women in frocks, who snapped their fingers at waiters who darted from the bar to table and back again, nimbly, almost invisibly, weaving through dancing couples, silver trays of drinks balanced expertly in hand.

Auguste Vaillant was dead, guillotined, even though he hadn't killed anyone. As Emile had predicted, the police were cracking down on the anarchists of Paris. Things were desperate. And all the while, these people get to laugh and dance and fuck, knowing full well that their joy is built on misery and death.

These people, Emile thought. Honestly. Worse than politicians, worse than police. At least politicians issued orders and the police did the dirty work, but these people... the rich. They did nothing.

Emile knew had glimpsed the future, witnessed

the rotten heart of it all, and he felt like a lone God gazing over the entire expanse of space and time knowing exactly where everyone had been, where everyone was now, and where everyone was going if someone didn't act now. If someone didn't rip the future from its roots.

Emile had never felt clarity like this. He was so shorn of futility and so full of purpose. He knew his mission now. He would not only avenge the tragedies of the past and the oppression of the present. He was going to save the future of anarchism from being lost to the nihilism of the future.

For that prize? For the future of anarchism?

Anyone was expendable. And everyone was guilty.

He was going to blow a hole in history.

He finished up his beer, paid, and left the café.

A couple of months later, a prosecutor at his trial asked him: 'Did you want to kill people at the Café Terminus?'

Emile fixed him with a cold grey stare, and replied: 'Certainly. As many as possible.'

As soon as the winter air hit him, Emile reached into his coat and pulled out a small kettle containing explosives, a detonator, a fuse and one hundred and twenty pellets. He lit the fuse with the cigar, shoved the door back open and threw the bomb into the Café and ran.

Moments later. The smoke settling. The waltz had been replaced by discordant cries and weeping. A woman held her face in her hands, blood seeping between her fingers; a waiter writhed on the floor, breathing in staccato bursts, pellets and splinters dug deep into his belly.

One person died as a result of Emile's attack. Dozens injured.

Emile was arrested after a brief chase.

The Café Terminus was open for business by the next afternoon.

At his trial, Emile made no attempt to excuse his

actions. He had no wish for forgiveness from a system he loathed, or for acts he didn't regret. And so, early one morning in May 1894, the moon still bulging in the sky, Emile Henry was executed by guillotine.

He was twenty one.

*

The embers of the squat party pulse, glow and recede with diminishing enthusiasm, before, finally, fading into ashes of silence.

The police have come, told everyone to shut up, and gone.

Alicia stirs and realises she's one of those left behind. Most other people have gone whooping like banshees into the city towards after parties or gone home to crawl under their quilts.

The remnants of the party are scattered around her, twitching furtively in half dreams on the soft things they've cobbled together for makeshift beds.

The comedown shame creeps on and she tries to

steady her mind with the mantra: Tea, toast, bed, tea, toast, bed, tea, toast, bed.

Alicia stands, grabs what she thinks are her things and asks the most conscious person to let her out. They open the metal door and she steps into the alleyway, scrunching her eyes at the winter morning even though it's a pale grey.

The alleyway. Compared to the ecstatic chaos of just hours before now looks so drab and every day. Crushed beer cans; broken wine bottles; spliff roaches mashed into puddles; baggies with shards of powder stubbornly clinging to them; the uniform, plain, damp brickwork; the monotonous dripping of the drainpipe; the kicked over bin, its spilt brown and grey contents exuding a ripe stench which broils in her stomach and bowels and all makes the previous hours seem so pointless, meaningless, and she thinks why the fuck do I always do this to myself, why the fuck do I always do this what a waste of fucking time, what a fucking waste of time –

No, no, no... Tea toast bed tea toast bed tea toast bed.

But despite the mantra she can't help but ask herself: is this is it? Is this it? After all the revolutions, the martyrs, the strikes, the occupations, the assassinations, the lines in the sand and the blood on the street... is this it? This one pathetic grey drizzly moment sandwiched between the vicarious thrills of dead white anarchists and the debris of the drug fucked? Is this it?

Tea toast bed tea toast bed tea toast bed.

She forces the answer out of herself. No. It can't be. It never has been. There's always more, there's always so much more.

But the bombs still go off. And tomorrow always comes.

Hood up, head down, she hurries into the future.

**III**

## Molotov

Find a bottle. Glass one. Yeah, that'll do.

See?

Through it, consider the smudged world.

Pour the petrol. Steady. Don't spill it for fuck's

sake. Focus.

Nerves're for those who've got the time.

Douse that rag.

Mind your hands.

You'll need em for the consequences.

Jam it in.

Make sure there's plenty poking out.

Don't let chance decide.

Pull your arm back.

Cover your face from the smoke.

Choices come to us like choking.

Let it burn.

# Cold Against My Fingers

It's the day before payday.

and I can already feel

the copper and silver

cold against my fingers,

and hear notes of rapture

hummed from cash machines.


Ever gone to work skint?

There's a heaviness to it.

It drags your feet,

buckles your knees,

hangs tiny weights from your heart.


The day curdles

with cosmic dissonance,

a scrunched up toothpaste tube

squeezed of life,

a class war we lose

at the end of each month.

So it's not greed, you understand,
this talk of money.
It's more desperate,
more feral than that.

So I hold on to that tomorrow
like something so precious like

Terrence, thirty-four years old, who's handcuffed
to the bed, face down in a pillow, his whole world
darkness and softness and gorgeous, sharp pain as
he's pegged by his wife, who slaps his arse, the
burn of a razor fingernail slashing a buttock,
followed by the warm trickle of blood, but he
doesn't care, ensconced in the all-engulfing
pummel and twinge and throb of being bound and
fucked. The dildo hammering his prostate brings
him a joy that only expresses itself in ball-gagged

squeals and grunts, and the orgasm bulges, a star
on the brink of supernova. This is his birthday
present, he doesn't know if he'll ever get this again,
and so he scrabbles around in his mind to horde
this moment for a lonely night and

I hold on like that
like something so precious
something so raging like

Hannah, sixteen years old, whose anger is an
incoherent howl in the dark of her stomach, but it
pulses with meaning. She creeps into the industrial
estate on the outskirts of town, petrol can in hand.
There's an abandoned building, six stories high,
fire exit off its hinges. She squeezes through the
gap. The ground floor is littered with an age of junk.
Perfect kindling. She opens the petrol can and
pours until it's empty. She steps out the fire exit,
strikes a match, tosses it in, running now, the

crackle and whoosh behind her, to the park and up the hill from where she watches the flames silently hold the building like a kind of love, like a cleared debt, and in that moment she knows how fragile the world is, how powerful she can be, and she embraces that knowledge and

I hold on like that
like something so precious
like something so raging
like something so desperate like

Anita, eight years old, who's cajoling her brother, Pawan, to take her to the park. Their Mum shoots Pawan a look. What Pawan can't let on, of course, is that he's really stoned. So Pawan rolls his eyes, huffs, slips on his trainers and walks with Anita to the park, finding a spot by the riverside. On glorious days like this, the sunlight on the water's surface splits like panned gold. And as Anita plays

in the shallows of the river, Pawan settles under the
cool shade of a tree. And as she goes knee deep into
the water, his eyelids are fluttering under the
weight of his stoned haze. And as she practices her
swimming, he's asleep, and soon Anita is
drowning, her mouth filled with water and weeds,
plugging her screams, and she grips that gold
though it breaks in her tiny hands and

I hold on like that

on the day before payday.
It's the only thing that stops me
collapsing with exhaustion from
skipping through the zeros
that noose each moment,

and on the way home from work,
the evening aching with a lack of promise,
the unreachable stars shine like newly minted coins

but I keep my eyes to ground

and march on.

# My Armour

Stirring to the shrill of the siren, my eye crust splits at the seams.

Breakfast, coffee, wash, shave. Then I put on my armour. It's weakened by rust and spattered with dried blood. Needs a clean but it'll have to do. No time.

At the transport point others wait with me and through their armour I sense a muzzled fear. The convoy pulls up, doors rasping open. We shuffle on. Like every morning, I think of escape. Too much of a risk. I take my seat. The engine's grumble only serves to underscore our frayed silence.

Inside my armour, my breath roars.

The convoy reaches my destination. I alight at the fringes of the battleground. The distant disembodied screams; the billowing stench of smoke and blood. I have no idea what happens to those who stay on the convoy, and they will have no idea what happens to me.

I gather pace on approach. Entering the battleground, some are already slain, lolling tongues dotted with flies, guts hanging out. There's a few writhing wounded. One of them grabs my leg, screaming for help. I kick them away and hurry on.

The battle itself is a fleeting, pitiless blur. Nothing to dwell on. Nothing to mourn.

As the sun is brushed away by dusk, the battle ends. I head back to the transport point, leaving the dead and dying where they fall. My armour is spattered with fresh blood. I should clean it on my return, but in my exhaustion, I know I will leave it to rust.

At the transport point, unknown survivors from unknown battles gather with me, waiting. We're alive, but we reek of defeat.

## Work Event

No thanks,

my whole life is an escape room.

# Notes on Faking Your Own Death

## RUCKSACK

1 x tooth brush

1 x toothpaste (100ml)

1 x shower gel (100ml)

2 x t shirts, pants, socks

1 x jumper

1 x anorak

1 x shorts

2 x good books

Flip flops

Tobacco, rizla, filter, lighter

I-pod (nb delete nostalgic songs)

Earphones (splash out on DECENT pair)

Passport

## TO DO

Print boarding pass

Withdraw cash

Change money

Clean flat

Keep going to work until last mo (CONSISTENCY)

**DO NOT DRINK**


## CAT

Clean litter tray

Put out few days food/water

Cuddle

Try and explain


## LAST TIME SEEING PEOPLE

Carry on as NORMAL

DO NOT get teary eyed

DO NOT hug goodbye for too long

They will NEVER understand

## SUICIDE NOTE

Google: suicide notes (inspiration)

Unconditional love for friends, family etc etc etc

Tone of complete resignation/desperation

Avoid clichés


## LAST DAY

Leave keys on side

Leave back door unlocked


DO NOT look back

## Ideation

Catch myself

floating in my pint

face down,

arms outstretched,

frozen for help.

I peer up into the amber.

Eyes drunk on terror.

Body bloated.

Blueberry lips.

I down it all

before anyone notices.

## Another Attempted Suicide in Temporary Accommodation

Staff find him at checks.

Hole in his sock,

big toe a heartbeat from

the fading carpet.


They're shocked,

but surprise

isn't in their job description.


Dosette box,

empty tins,

blackened pipe.

Same difference.


Politely ignoring that

he's shat himself

brown and red,

they cut him down,

ring 999.


*is he breathing*


*i don't know*


*put your ear to his lips*
*and follow my instructions*


When he's stretchered

down the stairs

the walls tick tock

with cheap lighters.


Staff promise his keyworker

they'll keep the room open

for when he's feeling better.

## The Marine

The bus pauses for a little too long at its stop. From the top deck, I hear voices wind up the stairs. There's a drunk guy trying to get on the bus. American, I think. Begging the driver for a free ride. There's something broken in his voice, and his meekness is no match for the bus driver's bluntness.

– Not today mate. Fuck off.

The doors hiss shut, muting the man's rambling apologies. I tentatively peer out of the window. His face is lowered, his shoulders hunched. He slumps down on the bright red plastic seat like a forgotten puppet, hopelessly wait in the dim glow of the bus shelter.

He slides out of view as the bus pulls away. I space out at the fading evening.

\*

A few hours later. I'm waiting for the night bus to

ferry me back. I check, double check, triple check the bus timetable and light a cigarette every time a bus arrives that isn't mine.

I feel his presence behind me a moment before his slurred American accent prickles my neck. I turn and see his face for the first time. His skin battle cracked beyond age. Despite his drunkenness, he isn't tottering or swaying. He stands with a studied straightness, and his eyes stare into mine with a distant confidence.

He asks me for a pound so he can get a beer.

– No mate.

He looks down for a moment, then fixes me with a renewed intensity.

He tells me he's a marine.

And then he tells me he wants to die.

– Why?

He tells me because he's killed too many men.

The silence falls like a guillotine.

I try to comprehend the cold pain in his bones

but I can't. The useless words drizzle out of me.

– I'm sorry.

With a single resigned nod, he turns and drifts away, his future weighed down by unnumbered corpses. He shrinks into the darkness until there's nothing left.

My bus arrives and I head straight to the top deck.

I stare at nothing as the bus shudders away, taking me back to the bright, comfortable, careless world where the dead don't exist, and ghosts can only be found in stories.

## Drive

Doing eighty down the A1. Rings

of fumes trail me. Last rites

circle my dreams like vultures – mean

twitching silhouettes that know

my hour

has come. Here's the point:


There comes a point

where living wrings

you out like a cheap hour.

Find yourself flapping, slick with oil, right

on the shore, blind. No

idea what it means.


Doing eighty down the A1. I mean

where do you find the point

when the world looks so sharp; knows

how to burst the protective ring

you've etched around your feet, writes

your to-do list and burns it within the hour.


What was our

land whips past me. A mean

of my dreams and past struggles: the rights

we settled for, the point

lost as the flames burn rings

in the singed marshmallow clouds. What I know


is broken. What I know

is a week crumbled into hours

scattered in rings

around minutes, means

of escape dashed in seconds, the point

battered in with every blink, right


now: doing 90 on the A1. I write

my future in concrete streams and know

the hectic, calamitous points

that ushered me to this hour,

the chaos that gnaws the means

of hope and vomits the Hell we wring.


I stumble on the point at the last moment; right

between the ring road and only what I know:

that the hours I lived were lost to the means.

# Bare Knuckle Fight in a Lidl Car Park

Security paid off to keep their mouths shut. They
leave for an extended fag break, high vis twinkling
in the distance
before being swallowed by the dark like dying stars.

A countless number have flocked here. All manner
of folk huddled, hushed, jostling for warmth in the
dank depths of a Wednesday night. The skipper
marches through the crowd, bin bag held open.

'No weapons, no phones, you know the rules,' she
barks,
because we're bare knuckle fighting in a Lidl car
park.

When the skipper's not looking a few of us place
bets. Turnout, injured, body count. It's not strictly
permitted,

but the purists can't begrudge others trying to make a few extra quid in these trying times.

The wizened, quick-fingered bookies whisk through the crowd, scabbed fists bursting with notes, hissing: 'Take your bets now you feckless cunts the fight's about to start.' The countdown to a bare knuckle fight in a Lidl car park.

This is a ritual. It's what must be done. The first whistle blows and we form the traditional circle, concrete between us an abyss into which we pour our daily anxieties:

pre-paid meters running red as an abattoir floor;
security-tagged baby formulae;
the dread flutter of brown envelopes tumbling from letterbox to doormat;
a skinny man nodding out at the foodbank;
wincing at every contactless beep;

payslips burning in a monthly wildfire;

the stress, the stress,

the perennially curled fist of stress,

tight as the silence of war.

This is our communion, our invocation, an

acceptance of our charge before we bare knuckle

fight in a Lidl car park.

The skipper steps into the circle, whistle dangling

on her lanyard. She takes a final drag of her fag and

crushes it beneath her work boot. Surveys the

congregation, waits for silence.

'Now,' she says. 'We know why we're here, don't

we?'

Murmurs of assent from the crowd.

'It's time to pray.'

We bow our heads and the skipper begins.

'We are joined here to appease the forces that have

pledged us prosperity and stability. Forces as

powerful and natural as the sun that, not so long ago, we would pray to for harvest. We appease them for we have been forsaken. Our bank accounts fallen fallow. In this earthly realm, we have done as we can: emailed our bosses, cast our ballots. Yet our plates and cups remain empty. And so we must appeal to these forces directly with a sacrifice. A blood sacrifice. We call upon the souls of all those who have fallen before so that you may be prepared. Have strength. For not all of you will survive, but know that your blood has been spilled for a higher purpose.'

The rumbling black clouds swell with portents – hark! The whistle's second blow kicks off the bare knuckle fight in a Lidl car park.

No one is exempt. What matters is that we are all present
as we

punch, jab, slap,

pierce, puncture,

boot, batter,

bash, beat, break,

dislocate, crush,

mutilate, gouge

in a frenzy that knows no time. We lose ourselves in
the morass, melt into one, unified in purpose.

You can tell this is ancient, because dried blood is
the colour of bark as we bare knuckle fight in a Lidl
car park.

The whistle's final blow and we stop. It takes a
moment to adjust, to fade from the clarity of ritual
to the filter of our lives and truly survey the ruins:
the concrete and our ripped to rags clothes
spattered with blood, guts, teeth and brain;
scattered bodies twisted and broken in every
conceivable way. We return to our circle, howl to

the sky in honour of the departed.

We all do our bit to leave no trace. We wash away the gore. Designated first aiders rush to the scene. They do the best they can. We clean the grime from our skin with antibacterial wipes. Change into clean clothes. Bloodied items stuffed into bin bags, loaded into the backs of trucks for disposal. Location unknown.

It's then that we see them.

The spirits.

The spirits, rising from the corpses, translucent silver-gilt bubbles, rising and rising above the halo of security lights. We watch in quiet awe and wonder as they rive on the wind, bursting into moon-glittered shards before melting into the air. The emptied bodies crumble to dust.

We head home, silent strangers once more, and wait for change.

The oil spots in puddles tremble as our footsteps leave no mark. It's like nothing ever happened at the Lidl car park.

# This Happened And I've No Idea What It Means

They got rid of the bendy buses in London a while
back. People used to call them the free bus because
you could get in and out via a side door and not
have to tap your Oyster card. This freedom
attracted a diverse crowd, and with it, fractured the
London bus ride's usual contract of silence. Drunks
freely smoking spliffs at the back, feet dangling
over the seat in front; ravers, irises swallowed by
pupils, gabbled away; romances were sealed and
fights broke out. Transport for the wasted, lost,
lonely and mad.

I can't remember where I was going. I had my
earphones in, the music mingling with the engine's
rumble and hum. The bus stopped and the side
doors rasped open. A man and woman careened in,
both pissed, clutching open cans of strong Polish
lager. They looked like people in their thirties who

looked like people much older than their thirties. I snobbishly checked my watch. 11am. The man hung from one of the rubber grips attached to the roof. The woman was shouting at him, face scrunched by snarling rage, a booze-soaked anger that's convinced of its righteousness. I turned my music down.

- YOU FUCKING CUNT... YOU FUCK... YOU FUCKING CUNT

Her voice torn with tears. The man didn't reply, didn't move. Kept his eyes to the floor. He was motionless. I'd have thought he was dead if it wasn't for his hold on the rubber grip turning his knuckles pale.

- WHAT'VE YOU GOT TO SAY

Rumble, hum.

– WELL? YOU FUCKING CUNT

She lunged forward, shoving him in the shoulder. Lager splashed to the floor. Still, he said nothing, head bowed.

– YOU DON'T KNOW DO YOU YOU FUCKING CUNT, YOU HAVEN'T GOT A FUCKING CLUE

She lunged again, this time with hard slap to the cheek. His head snapped back like he'd been hit by a sniper, then nodded forward once more. Passengers gave up their furtive glances and now openly stared.

– YOU DON'T KNOW HOW IT FEELS, HOW IT FUCKING FEELS

She crushed the can, foaming lager running over her clenched fist, before throwing it at his face. He remained passive, hanging, silent. The woman's shout ripped into a ragged scream.

– I WAS FULL OF BLOOD. I WAS FULL OF BLOOD YOU FUCKING CUNT

This final throe struck her off balance, and she staggered back, saved only from falling by wrapping herself tight around a pole, a life raft in a howling ocean. Now spent, she could only glare at him, fierce eyes red and swollen with raging tears, catching her breath between sobs. The man did nothing.

We hung in space together.

The bus juddered to a halt. The man and the woman tumbled out the side doors as if shackled by the ankles, vanishing into the bedlam of afternoon shoppers.

We all carried on. I put my earphones back in and turned the music up as loud as it would go.

Anyway. That's what happened. And I've no idea what it means.

## Appreciation

From the hospital,
Mum's texting updates
on Grandpa's progress.

I try to imagine another thirty seven years and then
some;
try to imagine not even being halfway through;
try to fathom the shape of sheer dumb luck.

But those thoughts are too bright,
like the doors have been kicked in,
and I'm found naked,
shivering,
stripped of words.

## Hollow Hymns

This place is our final destination.

A shopping centre

slowly murdering us with boredom

with nothing but murmured muzak

and our haggard, baggy-eyed reflections for

company.

This place is where we roam:

for anything to hunt and gather

on these barren litter-beaten streets;

for any semblance of what came before

we were choked by our traded futures,

and no, we don't have the time

because it's all run out.

This place was skinned

leaving nothing but smooth bone.

No tombstones to gather moss.

No cave etchings or

*we wuz ere* scrawled hopelessly on the wall.

Just gaudy buy-one-get-one-free signposts

directing us to the remnants of our lives.


There's no energies to imbibe,

no tide of memories,

nothing blooms,

nothing dies,

and everything's too fucking clean

to glean any feeling.

There's nothing to search for any more,

no flecks of historical compost

to breathe thick into our lungs,


just glimpsed postcards

from an amnesiac vacuum.

Sometimes

there's twinkles of joy

but these never last long.

Feeling them most keenly in the brief

warm haze of shower masturbation

until the fuzzy shudder gives in

to self-loathing and remorse, and

the monotone tanoy intones in our heads:

*Thankyou, please come again.*


We're all stillborn tabla rasas,

meandering photoshopped pubs

in which bar staff,

struggling to find an adjective

for 'pretending to be happy',

robotically offer the mantra:

*fosterskronenbergorstella*

The jukeboxes only play songs

that are part of the furniture.

*fosterskronenbergorstella*

And the only furniture is soaked

into the wallpaper.

*fosterskronenbergorstella*

And the wallpaper is peeled and cracked.

*fosterskronenbergorstella*

*fosterskronenbergorstella*

*fosterskronenbergorstella*


I tap my card,

drinking only to lose

all the reasons why I'm drinking

with half-remembered friends

and half-forgotten fucks.

By chucking out time

we either end up in fights,

pointlessly thudding knuckles on chipped teeth;

or stagger into alleyways with strings of vomit

hanging out of our burning mouths;

or drive home,

blearily watching the flickering cinema road,

the same exhausted cliches blinking before us,

praying for a crash through the screen -

but unfortunately, we all arrive home safely,

drunken, undamaged, undead,

and our sleep is a snatched, blank reprieve

from the coma of waking.


On star starven nights,

lit only by floating orbish streetlights

and soundtracked by distant glass tinkling,

I climb through a broken window

of my old school

and wander across old, creaking horizons.

Blurs of boundless energy

shoot past me.

Distant lost virginities glimmer.

Sober scuffles flicker in videotape

on the edges of recollection.

Everything looks so fragile,

like a dying fire,

and I tip toe,

holding my breath,

a delicate tyrant,

scared that if I breathe too hard

everything I control will

crumble to ash.

But there's no control here,

just the illusion of choice,

and slowly the ashes stuff

my eyes and throat.


Helpless, I leave,

heading to what I think is still home,

or at least, it'll be shelter.


I look to escape this place,

but the bus and train timetables have become

ancient essays in dead languages.

The orbital noose tightens

and I stand at the border of everything,

screaming hysterics at electric fences.

This place is a never exploding bomb threat,

a burnt out church

with scorched parchment floating in the breeze.


I strain for hollow hymns

but hear nothing.


Nothing.


Except


the slick automatic sliding doors click,

and the whimpering

as the ghosts barely hang on

by their fingertips.

## Pact

The grass tickles our cheeks
under the yawning blue oblivion.

'We've got so little time, don't we?'
you say.

I nod,
slide my fingers between yours
and hold on.

## Spent

Accounts hollowed out,

overdrafts exhausted.

Direct debits, standing orders,

debts, loan repayments

emptied of meaning.

Trundle home

with a trolley full of booze

from the raided Waitrose,

docs crunching broken glass.

Dealers texted.

They arrive with

screeching wheels,

fast palms,

and are pleased with business tonight.

We agree we've talked enough

for a lifetime.

Turn it up.

Music clatters in our blood.

A scattered galaxy of records

on the burn-mottled carpet.

Our voices milk Hell,

scorched in shot glasses,

boots stamping tiny explosions,

but the neighbours won't complain

and the filth won't come knocking.

Not tonight.


The heaps of

gorgeous waste:

shreds of baccy,

torn off corners of kingskins,

twisted roaches,

drained bottles,

abused library cards,

upcycled banknotes,

mirrors smeared beyond reflection,

crumpled tissues blossoming crimson,

baggies wiped of all

but the most stubborn crystals.

That familiar itch,

old lovers working my heart.

We hold each other

and gabble sounds

like bare feet

stepping onto a beach.

Our fingers trace

the shifting grooves in our spines.

Sirens strip our breathes,

blue-white flashes

strobe our oblivion.


A tweeted video:

the road splits like wet paper,

ochre eyes glow in the depths.

A roar.

A flicker of tongue and flame.

Something reaches up.

The frame shudders.

Black.


The sky melts, dripping acid clouds.

Preening cranes and towers

creak and topple

into the flaming streets.

Screams on the air.

We feel it upon us.

Was bound to happen eventually, I guess.


Fuck it.

Who's racking up?

Some of these poems have appeared in other publications and forms:

'Pact' appears in *Life's Wonders* anthology, Black Pear Press (2023)

'Drive' is a sestina, commissioned by Loud Poets as part of their Return To Form series, 2022

'Bridges' was published by *Ink, Sweat and Tears* (2021)

'Dead White Anarchists' was performed as a storytelling theatre show between 2019 – 2021, directed by Emily Ingram

'Hollow Hymns' was recorded for Captain of the Rant vs Hair Explosion's EP, *Nudges, Whispers and Threats* (2012)

# Acknowledgements

I started performing spoken word in 2008, and hope to always write and perform in one way or another. For this, I'm indebted to the promoters and performers who helped shape me into the artist I am today. The opportunities you gave me were invaluable.

Thanks to Chris Watson and Gary Budden for their eagle-eyed editing work.

To Mum for all the love and support. To Sonja.

To all my grandparents. Rest in peace.

To Dad for giving me books that changed my world.

Dead White Anarchists was a solo theatre show, written and performed by myself. It was directed by

Emily Ingram, who was essential in helping create a piece of theatre I was proud to take around the country. Thank you. And thank you to everyone who supported the show.

And last, but by no means least, I owe an untold amount to all those who put me up, gave me rides, food, drinks, cigarettes and whatever else in my more wayfaring years. You know where I am if you you want to call it in.

# About the author

Paul Case is a writer and actor living in Edinburgh. He has performed his own poems and stories all over the UK and internationally since 2008. He has also written, performed and toured the solo theatre shows Dead White Anarchists (2019 - 2022) and Rogues So Banished (2024).

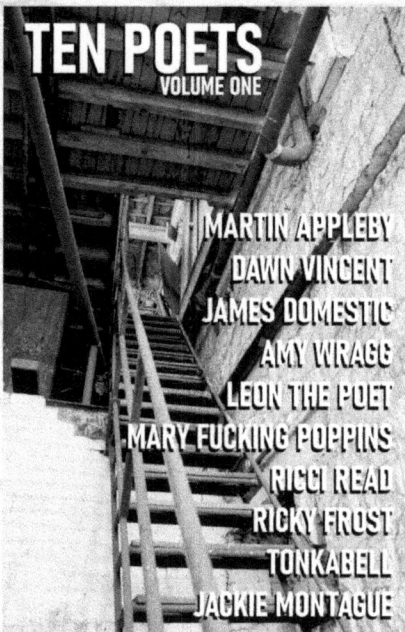

TEN POETS
VOLUME ONE

MARTIN APPLEBY
DAWN VINCENT
JAMES DOMESTIC
AMY WRAGG
LEON THE POET
MARY FUCKING POPPINS
RICCI READ
RICKY FROST
TONKABELL
JACKIE MONTAGUE

Ten Poets (Volume One)
by Martin Appleby, Dawn Vincent, James Domestic, Amy Wragg, Leon The Poet, Mary Fucking Poppins, Ricci Read, Ricky Frost, Tonkabell, Jackie Montague.

The first in a series of books showcasing poets of all stripes and intended to act as a primer to check out their other work and/or book them to perform in your city, town, or village.

Poetry is arguably in (another) period of renaissance right now – everyone and their dog is a poet; just check out Instagram or TikTok – but there's plenty of really terrible poetry around, as there always has been. We don't want that stuff; we want the diamonds that sparkle in the dirt, those that are using poetry to connect with audiences, to say something about the human condition, to make people think, reflect, and maybe even laugh like drains (poetry on some level is entertainment, and only an inveterate snob would say otherwise).

For some of the poets that feature in this collection, this is their first published work. For others, these poems sit alongside their other books, contributions to literary magazines etc. It doesn't matter; they're all here in one place and demanding your attention, so dive in and give them some!

Available at www.earthislandbooks.com

Old West

**TIME FOR MY GENERATION TO DIE**

by E.D. EVANS

Illustrations by Natalie Woolfson

E.D. Evans is a lifelong poet. Having spent time in both London and New York during Punk's original heyday in the late '70s and early '80s, Evans has always comfortably floated between those two worlds. She became deeply entrenched in New York's East Village art scene that was so pervasive in the 1980s/90s, spending years performing spoken word poetry at venues such as The Nuyorican Poets Café, Brownies, and The Knitting Factory. Her Instagram handle, @originalpunkster11 says it all.

"I've always liked to tell dark stories that rhyme, so hopefully my words translate into the ethos and audience for which it is intended. What a lot of young Punks today may not realize is that even back in the day, Punk was always about acceptance and inclusion. We were what we were—basically a bunch of creative misfits looking for our tribe, with a great soundtrack to boot. And when we found each other, it was a glorious thing."

Evans currently features her spoken word on social media platforms, and is collaborating with an array of visual artists and musicians to bring her poetry to life. She lives in the Sonoran Desert with parrots, a blind cat, lots of backyard lizards, and a madly talented multi-instrumentalist.

"...And to all our spokespeople who have passed, Rest in Punk. You influenced generations to come, and I, for one, will always be grateful."

Available at www.earthislandbooks.com

Andrea Janov books available from **E** **EARTH ISLAND BOOKS**

Andrea is a mess of contradictions, fan of parallel structure, and nostalgic pack rat who writes poetry about punk rock kids and takes photos of forgotten places. She believes in the beauty of the ordinary, the power of the vernacular, and the history of the abandoned. Through her work, she strives to prove that poetry can be dirty, gritty, and accessible by revealing the art in what we see, say, do, ignore, and forget every day.

Raised by rock and roll parents, she learned the importance of going to concerts and ignoring the "no trespassing" signs in her childhood. She spent her adolescence in a small town punk rock scene where she moshed, fell in love, and produced a few cut-and-paste zines, before escaping to New York City and causing a ruckus in Alphabet City. After meeting her husband in one of those Chelsea bars she has settled in Pittsburgh, is at the whim of a feisty terrier, works in tech, and still prefers Jameson neat.

After paying a few universities way too much tuition, they granted her several degrees in creative writing. When her education was complete, she started garnering some publishing credits, including a sold out run of her first book, 'Mix Tapes and Photo Albums: Memories from a small town scene'.
'Short Skirts and Whiskey Shots' picks up from where 'Mix tapes...' left off.

She is uncomfortable talking about herself, even in third person.
www.andreajanov.com

Available at www.earthislandbooks.com

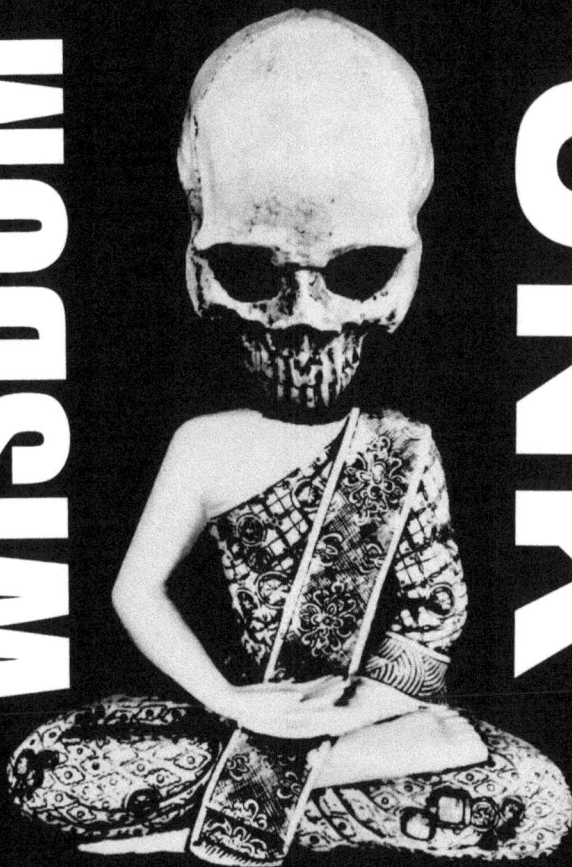

available from **Ei EARTH ISLAND BOOKS**

WISDOM OF THE PUNK BUDDHA

www.earthislandbooks.com

TEN POETS
VOLUME ONE

MARTIN APPLEBY
DAWN VINCENT
JAMES DOMESTIC
AMY WRAGG
LEON THE POET
MARY FUCKING POPPINS
RICCI READ
RICKY FROST
TONKABELL
JACKIE MONTAGUE

TEN POETS
VOLUME TW

JAMES DOMESTIC
MARY DICKINS
BARRY KING
LORNA MACKINNON
STUART WEBB
E.D. EVANS
SAM MARSH
DARREN J. BEANEY
DAVID CHIDGEY
LEA MARIE

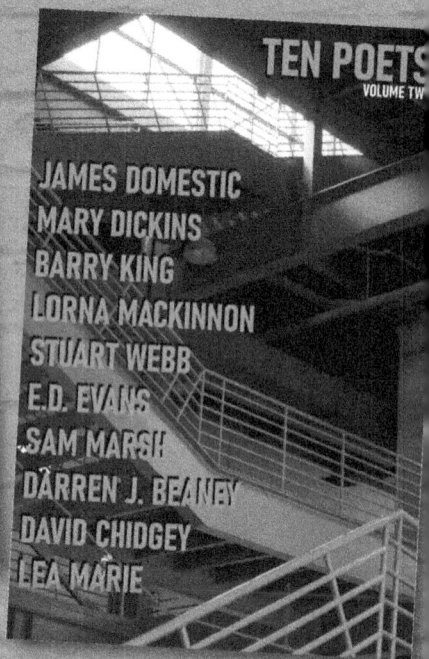

# TEN POETS VOLUME ONE & TWO

Poetry is everywhere and for everyone. Poetry paints pictures with words, tells stories, chews over ideas, can act as catharsis, can make you laugh like a lunatic, can make you cry tears of sorrow or joy, picks it the scabs of everyday life, ponders the absurd. Can be cruel, can be kind, can be full of passion - love and hate. Can be a catalyst for reflection, renewal, or revolution! Poetry is all these things and more. Poetry is our lingua franca.

For some of the poets that feature in these collections, this is their first published work. For others, these poems sit alongside their other books, contributions to literary magazines etc. It doesn't matter; they're all here in one place and demanding your attention, so dive in and give them some!

**Available at www.earthislandbooks.com**

9 781916 864504